*To Doris With Love,
From Woody Day*

To Doris With Love, From Woody Day

—My Days with Doris Day—

By Syd Wood

BearManor Media
2022

To Doris With Love, From Woody Day

© 2022 Syd Wood

All rights reserved.

No portion of this publication may be reproduced, stored, and/or copied electronically (except for academic use as a source), nor transmitted in any form or by any means without the prior written permission of the publisher and/or author.

Published in the United States of America by:

BearManor Media

4700 Millenia Blvd.
Suite 175 PMB 90497
Orlando, FL 32839

bearmanormedia.com

Printed in the United States.

Typesetting and layout by BearManor Media

ISBN—978-1-62933-873-6

Dedication

This dedication of my long overdue book is to a number of people who made up a big part of my life and contributed to the man I am today.

First and foremost, I thank my Dad and especially my Mom who introduced me to Doris Day as a young child in music and cinema. Once I heard that beautiful voice and saw the actress she was, I was completely enchanted. Who knew at the time that she would become such a vital part of my life for many, many years to come?

Even 'till this day, I'm stopped by people who ask me about my time with Doris, and encourage me to write a book about my years in her home and with her son Terry, who called me 'Woody Day. He was a brother to me and a great friend.

I dedicate this book to all my friends along the way who enjoyed Doris as much as I did, and who shared that love—wanting nothing from me but to share sweet memories.

I also dedicate this book to my husband, Scott Harley Wood, who has stood by me through good and bad times, has protected me at all costs, and has helped me get this book going. He is my rock.

Lastly, I want to thank a dear friend of mine, Lloyd Jessen, who unselfishly has taken personal time out of his busy life to help me put this book together. He is one of the kindest souls and I know Doris felt the same way.

Love and Best Wishes to All,
Woody Day

Table of Contents

Dedication..v

Chapter One..1

Chapter Two..5

Chapter Three...8

Chapter Four..11

Chapter Five...16

Chapter Six...20

Chapter Seven...23

Chapter Eight..25

Chapter One

I was born Sydney James Wood in England on July 2, 1941, in Kersey, Suffolk, in an area known as East Anglia. My father, John, was an officer in the British Air Force and my mother, Eliza, was a homemaker who loved going to the movies. I was the last of five children. I had one sister, Evelyn, and three brothers—John, William and Glenn. My brothers followed our father into the military; I chose a different path.

My birthplace—the little village of Kersey—is known for its picturesque main street with medieval timber-framed houses and a ford across a stream, known locally as "The Splash". St. Mary's Church crowns the hill at one end of the village, and the old post office—located inside a private house—sat at the opposite end of the street. I was born in that house.

When I was a young boy, my Mum and I would take frequent one-hour trips to Ipswich to see the films of the day in the Old Odeon Theatre located on Lloyd's Avenue. The theatre opened on September 7, 1936. *On Moonlight Bay* (1951) was most likely the first Doris Day movie I saw there, and I was instantly captivated by the beautiful, young lady who played Marjorie Winfield. *Calamity Jane* (1953) would later become my all-around favorite Doris Day movie, but I loved segments of all of her films.

My Mum would always say, "I like her (Doris), she's always kissing the men!" I loved the way Doris was always laughing or smiling or dancing in her films. It was everything my sister didn't do! With Doris, there was always happiness and joy, something we rarely had in my home.

When I was about 12, my family moved to Dagenham, a town in east London. There, I went to the theatre to see Doris Day films by myself, sometimes watching them two or three times in one sitting. There was something about Doris that just took hold of me.

I soon acquired a record player and spent all of my pocket money on Doris' recordings, which at that time were sold on 78's. I had to play catch-up, gradually collecting all the albums Doris had recorded earlier. I never grew tired of listening to her singing.

By 1969, I was on my own and working for a printing and photography business in London. Along with three other Doris Day fans, we formed a group that came to be known around the world as the "Doris Day Society." It was created with Doris' express permission and blessing. Along with Denis Hoffman, John Rainer, and Sheila Smith, I helped launch a quarterly *Doris Day Society Journal* beginning in March 1970. In the first issue, I wrote:

Hello and Welcome,

This is it—our very first 'DAY' journal and I must say here and now how happy and proud I am to be a part of it.

My official title is Secretary. In brief this means I shall be handling the advertising, dealing with membership and subscriptions, and also answering any urgent inquiries, and I stress URGENT.

In future editions of the magazine, there will be a 'Question & Answer' service. Its purpose: to cover each and every query and enquiry received between journals, thus avoiding unnecessary correspondence which you realize is very costly and time consuming.

Like other Dayniacs, I'm in love with Doris Day, the woman, the voice … even those fabulous freckles. There is no other entertainer around with that special magic, a magic of which our Doris has plenty.

In the months and years to follow, I'm willing to share with you one of the world's finest stars who is at the top of her profession.

This is your Society—your magazine. Let us hear from you.

Best Wishes,
Sydney Wood

In that same first issue of the *Doris Day Society Journal*, Doris provided the following letter, dated December 9, 1969:

> Sorry I have taken so long in answering your letter but television keeps me going every minute of the day. I am enjoying the show this year very, very much but I shall look forward to my vacation in the spring.
>
> I wish that I had more time to write a long, newsy letter but they shall no doubt be calling me to the set any minute, so I have to make it brief.
>
> Just wanted you to know that I enjoyed hearing from you and am so happy to know that the club is doing well. Please give my very warm "hello" to all the members and thank them for their interest in me and my work. I truly do appreciate it.
>
> Again, thank you and may I wish you everything good in the New Year: Peace, health and happiness.
>
> Sincerely,
Doris

By June 1970, Denis Hoffman had been replaced by Valerie Andrew as an officer of the Society. In a letter dated March 12, 1970, Doris again corresponded with the club:

> Received the copy of the *Society Journal* and I think it's just super. All the pictures are really good ones and thank you for being so discriminating in selecting them. It's really and truly well done and I commend you highly for this. Please pass on to all the members my gratitude and thanks for such a fine *Journal*.
>
> The article written by Denver Pyle was incredible to say the least. I didn't know that he had done an interview with you; or did you get it from a newspaper? How nice of him to say those things, but of course, I feel the same way about him, so the feeling is mutual. If, when the next *Journal* comes out you would like to send a list of questions to me to be answered, I would be

happy to do so. Also, perhaps you would like a story from Rosemarie and a few of the other members of the cast. You can let me know about that, too.

This is just a brief note as I don't have much time right now, but I wanted you to know how I felt about the *Journal*. Thank you, thank you—all of you for such a fabulous *Journal* and my love and warmest wishes to everyone.

Doris

Chapter Two

On September 14, 1973, a headline in the *Daily Express* announced "Actress Doris Day comes to London for the first time in fifteen years at the end of this month." My initial feelings of excitement gave way to doubt. I had lived through this type of rumor before.

But on Friday evening, September 21, while I was on my way home from work, I opened that day's newspaper and saw a huge photo of Doris arriving at Heathrow Airport the day before, accompanied by her good friend, author Jacqueline Susann. The headline read "Doris Has Her Day in London."

The next day, I received a phone call from another fan who lived in London, who suggested that we should try to meet Doris. At first, I rejected the idea, fearing Doris might consider it an unwelcome intrusion. But then the more I thought about it, I changed my mind and went to the Dorchester Hotel in Mayfair, where Doris was staying.

When I entered the lobby, the first person I saw was the famous American composer, songwriter, and pianist Burt Bacharach. I paused and watched him for a few moments. Then I looked off to the side, and saw Doris sitting at a table in front of the lobby windows. My heart raced and I felt a slight panic take hold of me. I timidly walked up to her and said, "Hi, Doris, I'm Sydney!"

Doris instantly burst into a huge smile, jumped up, hugged me, and made a lovely fuss over me. I wiped tears away from my eyes and tried to calm myself. She and I really hit it off. After we had a long talk, Doris suggested that I bring a small group of fans to her hotel suite to meet with her later.

I phoned Sheila and together we made a list of about 17 people to invite. Our group met with Doris at the Dorchester the following Wednesday, September 26, at 6:45 pm.

Doris' friend from the U.S., Raquel Rael, served champagne and hors d'oeuvres. Doris was radiant, dressed in red pants and sweater, white shirt, and red shoes. She greeted each person with a warm smile and a kiss, and gave everyone California chocolates and bubble gum. She also shared her "Mom's Brag Book" which contained photos of her eleven babies: Biggest, Muffy, Charlie, Tiggy, Bubbles, Bobo, Bambi, Bucky, Daisy June, Schatzie, and Rudi. For two hours, Doris graciously took questions from our group, signed autographs, and posed for photos with everyone.

On Friday evening, September 28, I and a few other fans sat with Doris in the lobby of the Dorchester. Doris preferred the lobby to her suite, saying she thought it was more fun. She suggested changes that she'd like to make to the hotel's color scheme and thought there should be a dog seated on every chair. She even sang her own words to the tune of "I Love Paris" and made all of us laugh. On Saturday, September 29, Doris flew home to California.

Just three days later, on October 2, Sheila and Valerie were on their way to the U.S., flying first to New York, then onto St. Louis, and finally to Los Angeles. While in LA, they spent a lot of time with Doris and her mother, Alma, and formed an affectionate bond with them.

After spending time with Doris in London, I was on the phone with her every two to three weeks, discussing the *Doris Day Society Journal* and other matters. We became very close. Gradually, Doris came to trust and rely on me, Sheila and Valerie for much more than the British fan club.

On April 14, 1976, Doris married Barry Comden in Monterey, CA. They had met at the Old World Restaurant in Beverly Hills in May 1975 and by the end of that year Barry had moved in with her. It was a whirlwind romance. Doris proclaimed to the world that they were young and in love, and had a beautiful relationship.

In July 1976, Valerie and Sheila moved to Beverly Hills to work for Doris and Barry. I remained in England and continued to write, print, and distribute issues of the *Doris Day Society Journal.* Our last issue was released in the winter of 1977. Between 1970 and 1977, we published 30 issues which totaled 294 pages.

Chapter Three

In 1978, Doris invited me to come visit her. I stayed several weeks and spent most of my time at her house. I bathed, fed, and played with Doris' dogs; fixed her swing; and cleaned the gas lamps around her pool. Doris and I also did some gardening together. I showed her how to pick the dead heads off flowers, something Doris had never done before.

As I was getting ready to return to England, Doris said "Why don't you stay here and work for me?" I explained to her that I couldn't leave my father alone in London, following the death of my mother. I kept in touch with Doris and Barry by sending them cards and notes.

On Sunday, April 8, 1979, Doris wrote to me. She said that she and Barry had been thinking about when I should move to California, but they felt I should wait a bit. "We are so fond of you and would feel very happy to have you with us, but perhaps the timing is not quite right at the moment," she said.

Later in 1979, my Dad passed away. Soon thereafter, Doris called me and said, "Syd, pack your bags and come over."

I accepted Doris' offer and left England for America. I had two tours of duty with her which totaled nearly 20 years. My first period of service began in 1979 and ended around 1992. I later returned to work for Doris again in 2000 and stayed until 2004.

When I arrived in Los Angeles, Doris still lived at 713 Crescent Drive in Beverly Hills. She immediately told me: "You'll have to follow me around, I'm like a butterfly—I flit from one thing to another." I found that to be true. The dogs were always a big part of everything we did. She loved giving them funny names.

Throughout my time with Doris, I was employed as her personal assistant, bodyguard, and closest confidante. I performed various tasks and cared for her numerous animals. I did literally everything from bleaching Doris' hair, to altering her jeans, to making her bed, to answering the phone.

I also did a lot of housekeeping, cleaning, and gardening work for Doris. I would shop for flowers for her yard, at places like Kmart and Home Depot. She would tell me to buy whatever I liked. She was not a micromanager and she trusted my judgment.

Doris and I became best friends. I quietly did my job and always respected her space. She knew where I was when she needed me.

I was with Doris on Crescent Drive in 1979 when she received a surprise package from England one day. Warwick Records had released a vinyl album of some of her hit recordings the year before under the CBS label, and it was very popular. When we opened the box, we were amazed to see a framed album with a colourful inlay of the Union Jack in the upper left-hand corner. An inscription in the lower, right-hand corner read:

Presented to Doris Day by Interworld Music, Ltd., to recognize the outstanding sales in the United Kingdom of the Warwick long playing album "Doris Day 20 Golden Greats" 1979.

Doris was speechless. She loved her British fans and treasured the memories she had of her two trips to England. I was so pleased that she was recognized in this way and that the people of the United Kingdom still held her in such high regard.

Good times, such as this event, were mixed with unhappiness. During my first year with Doris, I watched her and Barry grow further and further apart. It was painful for me to witness. Increasingly, Barry would be away at his club all day. Sometimes, when Doris and I would be working in the garden, we'd look up and see him returning to the house. She'd turn to me and say, "Oh look, here comes the horse's ass." Sadly, her dislike of him kept growing and eventually she completely ignored him.

Barry was always pleasant to me, but he wasn't around all that much. He would bring his little boy, Danny, over to Doris' house to swim in her pool once a week.

Living with a famous person was a big adjustment for me. I hid in the trees whenever I heard a Beverly Hills tour bus approaching. Half the time they'd sit out front, with the tourists singing "Que Sera, Sera." I thought it was embarrassing.

One day, a man came to Doris' gate with a black and white bird in a large cage. As I began speaking to him, Doris walked up, opened the gate and invited him in. She fell in love with the bird and persuaded the man to leave it with her. Doris and I even posed for a photograph with the bird. Things always seemed to go her way and I had another animal to care for!

For me, working for Doris wasn't about the money. I was earning around $7.00 an hour when I first started, which wasn't much. But all of my living expenses were paid for by Doris. I never knew what a bill was like until I quit working for her.

Chapter Four

When it was time for Doris to move from Beverly Hills to Carmel in November 1981, Terry and I flew up together first. Doris' new home was an 11-acre sprawling, cliff-top, compound known both as 'Overlook' and 'Casa Loco.' The property looked over the 18-hole Quail Lodge Golf Course below. It was an idyllic setting filled with oak and buckeye trees; shimmering blue lupines and gold poppies grew wild in the meadows.

I moved into the gatehouse by Carmel Valley Road and Terry stayed in the guest cottage that Doris had built on the property. The following day five vehicles, 18 dogs, and Doris arrived at Overlook. The dogs were all shapes and sizes. There were golden retrievers, Labradors, poodles and dachsies. They all had names and they all knew who they were.

In their new home, the dogs each had their own rooms and they all had their own areas. Adjacent to the garage there was an area where the dogs had their own garden and backyard. They were all strays—animals that people didn't want. But they were really wonderful animals. They were happy because they could do whatever they wanted to do. When Doris would appear, they would go crazy. They'd nearly knock her over and she'd play with them all day.

After moving to Carmel, Doris focused all of her time and energy on helping the animals. She ran a 24-hour dog rescue operation from her home. She never turned down a stray dog. All newcomers would be checked out by a veterinarian and then boarded on Doris' property. If one of the dogs became ill, I would make arrangements for additional veterinary care and would only notify Doris if there was bad news.

Doris would become emotionally undone if a dog got sick. She always took such news very hard. Her Christian Science books would go flying across her bedroom whenever a dog died.

Although Doris was famous, I found her to be one of the most down-to-earth ladies I'd ever met. She had a washing machine in her bedroom, so she could easily do her own laundry. She often ironed her own clothes and considered herself the best at it. If you gave her a broom, you couldn't take it away from her. She loved sweeping! She'd take it off me if I was outside with it.

Doris took great pride in running her house well. She was always making and receiving phone calls, going out to breakfast or lunch, and taking the dogs for walks. She never stopped keeping busy, she just kept on the move all the time. I hardly ever saw her sit down. She was a content person.

Doris was a prolific writer of notes and lists that she would hand off to me or other workers for follow-up. She would use any scrap of paper that she might find near her and would write with pencil or ink pens of various colours. Oftentimes she would scratch through an item after reconsidering things.

Doris' grocery lists were very specific. They always included lots of fresh vegetables for both her and the dogs. Ice cream was her dessert of choice. Her favourite flavours were coffee/heath bar and Cherry Garcia˙. She often did her own marketing at either Safeway or Albertson's on Carmel Valley Road and would drive herself.

In those days Doris had a 4-door, V-8, white Jeep Grand Wagoneer, with wood panelling on the sides and rear. Her license plate holder read "Happiness is Being Single." One bumper sticker proclaimed "Abuse an Animal … Go to Jail!" Another asked "Have you hugged your best friend today?"

Once, while in the pet food aisle at Safeway, Doris literally bumped carts with actress Betty White. They spent several minutes chatting about dog food and drew a large crowd of curious spectators.

Doris would frequently leave housekeeping instructions for me and my co-workers, reminding us to clean certain areas or open specific windows. She was always very aware of things that needed attention.

I worked closely with a lovely woman named Meg Howard and we made a great team. As Doris' collection of dogs grew, I would walk all of them. In the early '90s, Doris had as many as 50 or more dogs. They even had their own kitchen.

When Doris and I worked together in the dog kitchen, she would often be in her house coat with her hair up, deboning chickens for the dogs. I routinely watched Doris sitting on a tall stool, picking the freshly cooked chicken apart. She went through it like a sieve, removing all the bones, fat and skin.

I would look at her face and think to myself, "God, when I was a kid, that face and that voice cost me all of my pocket money, buying her 78s, 45s and albums. Now, here I am today, standing next to her, and she's really no different than anyone else."

When I was in the dog kitchen with Doris, I'd sometimes start singing one of her songs. I would tell her when she recorded it and that would help bring it back to life for her. She would then remember the song and finish singing it. It was always such a sweet experience for me.

Doris kept the same household staff with her for decades and treated them as close friends, until about the last fifteen years of her life. Whenever Doris and her employees would disagree on anything, Terry stepped in as the negotiator and peace-maker. He was a buffer between the workers and Doris.

If anyone wanted a raise, Terry would talk to his mother about it first. When it came to staff salaries, Doris remembered that she only made $300 a week when she started working at Warner Bros. She could easily lose her temper over money. Doris usually gave only modest gifts to her employees. In 2003, her Christmas gift to me was a check for $200.

Doris was not the type of person who wanted to show off or reminisce about what she'd done in life; however, she was a perfectionist. Whenever we discussed her movies, she would always say "I could have done it better!"

Her mementos of her previous life in Hollywood were kept hidden away, wrapped in tissue. Doris had literally hundreds of memorabilia such as gold discs, billboard chart awards, trophies, magazine covers, and many other items which were all kept in boxes in a spare room.

On a typical morning at Overlook, Doris would come down to the kitchen in her dressing gown and make herself a ham sandwich or have a bowl of cereal, along with coffee or hot chocolate, depending on her mood. Then she'd feed the animals some little biscuits and prepare their main breakfast meal.

Although Doris had a love of food, she maintained a healthy diet. She never really ate all that much, and she'd always work off whatever she ate. She never put on weight; she was always the size she was during her heyday in Hollywood.

Doris would usually feed her dogs their dinner around 4:30 p.m., and then go over to her bedroom to eat a snack and watch TV. She watched a lot of British TV and loved Judi Dench. She also loved the British comedy *As Time Goes By*, which she thought was very well written. By 9:00 p.m., she would be in bed and ready to go to sleep. Seven or eight dogs would sleep in her bedroom with her.

Despite her low-key lifestyle, Doris still had her fair share of famous friends. She had calls from celebrities like Ronald Reagan, Rock Hudson, and Ginger Rogers. When she still lived in Beverly Hills, she confided in me that she hoped Lucy (Lucille Ball) wouldn't invite her to one of her famous card parties. Lucy smoked like a chimney and Doris hated inhaling it, even though she'd been a smoker herself.

Doris often had visitors in Carmel. She loved it when Betty White came to visit. Betty came four or five times for lunch – once when she was working on her book. She lived up on a cliff, near the beach in Carmel. I never met anyone who was more of a lady than Betty. She was always beautiful, and she kept a tissue wrapped up in her jacket cuff. When she would arrive, I would open the gates and tell her to drive down to the circle by the main house. But she would always insist that I get in the car and ride with her.

Dom DeLuise also visited Doris several times. He was a basket-case the first time. He, too, would insist that I get in the car and ride with him to Doris' front door.

In May 1983, Rock Hudson came up to Carmel to do a week of interviews with Doris on *Good Morning, America* for ABC-TV. At that point, they were talking about doing a sequel to their 1959 romantic comedy, *Pillow Talk*. When Rock arrived, he still looked very much like a 'Star'—extremely handsome, greying at the temples, with a face that could be carved in stone.

Doris had the greatest fun with Rock—he would joke with her all the time. He used to call her 'Eunice' and she called him 'Ernie.'

Pillow Talk-2 was going to be about how the two of them, after being divorced, were coming together again for the marriage of their child. Rock's character (Brad) had fallen in love again with Doris' character (Jan); and Tony Randall's character (Jonathan) had placed a bet that Brad couldn't get her back. The two men each bet a car. Unfortunately, the sequel was never made.

In the Fall of 1984, I helped Doris recover from her second facelift. The plastic surgeon lifted the skin on her forehead, around her neck, and under her chin. Doris healed quickly and was back to her regular routine within weeks.

When Doris agreed to do her *Best Friends* cable show on the Christian Broadcast Network in 1985, she asked Rock to be her first guest. She had no idea that he was so ill. When Rock arrived for the press conference at Pebble Beach, Doris didn't recognize him. Rock's segment aired on CBN after he died, so Doris did an announcement at the beginning of the program and became emotional when she spoke about him.

Chapter Five

Around 1992, I left Doris' employment and moved to Green Cove Springs, Florida. She and I had been getting on each other's nerves, and I felt it was time for a change. While living in Florida, I began making Doris Day wall clocks for friends and Doris' fans in England.

While I was away, Doris received a call from John Denver on October 11, 1997. He asked her to go out for dinner with him the following day. She agreed. While she was getting ready to meet him the next day, she heard the news that he had been killed when his homebuilt plane crashed in Monterey Bay near Pacific Grove. She was totally devastated. She talked about it for many years afterward. Doris and John cared deeply for each other. They had a remarkable bond. At one point, their relationship even went as far as them checking into a hotel together under assumed names. That was endearing to me since it made Doris all the more real—it made her just like the rest of us.

In 1999, Terry invited me back to Carmel for a visit, and he and Doris asked me to return to work for them. I ultimately agreed and returned in 2000. My primary job was to take Doris to lunch, *every* day.

One day, after my return to Carmel, I was passing through the garage when I heard the house phone ring. I picked it up and the voice on the other end said, "Hello, is Doris there?" I said, "She's walking dogs around the property—can I take a message?" The caller replied: "Yes, please tell her Paul called. Paul McCartney." He could hear my accent and asked if I was from England.

Paul and I then talked about Britain for about 20 minutes until Doris came in. I told her "Paul McCartney is on the phone," and Doris said, "Oh come on.

Somebody is pulling your leg." When Doris got on the phone, she talked for about an hour. Upon ending the call, she exclaimed to me, "That *was* Paul McCartney!" Paul was in LA at the time and he and his then-wife, Heather Mills, had been up the night before watching TV and saw Doris in *Calamity Jane* (1953).

The next week, I went down to the Albertson's grocery store in Carmel to escort Paul's limousine back to Doris' house. Paul bought Girl Scout cookies and also a little potted plant for Doris. Before Paul arrived, Doris told me, "He's only going to be here for about an hour." Much to my amazement, Paul and Heather ended up staying for over five hours. Paul asked me to take a picture of him and Heather with Doris. They hugged when they said their goodbyes. Paul loved Doris' property and what she'd done with it.

Paul invited Doris to come visit him in the UK, saying he'd send a private plane to fetch her. But Doris turned him down. Paul would telephone her often. He never paid attention to whether it was day or night in California, so he would sometimes awaken Doris in the middle of the night, just to say he was thinking of her. She got a kick out of that. Paul's friendship helped ease Doris' loneliness, and she looked forward to his calls.

I remember Doris as always being incredibly beautiful. She would go over to the bathroom on her side of the house and come back two hours later, looking like a million dollars! Her face would be made up—but not overly so. Her hair would be blonde and flowing—she'd have a straw hat on, and she looked absolutely fantastic. She never lost her gorgeous smile. I always said to her, "You're going to live forever, you'll outlive everyone." And she'd just laugh and tell me to stop being silly.

Doris would often tell me that she had the personality of her character in *Calamity Jane* (1953), and she did. But I felt she was more like the character she played in *It Happened to Jane* (1959). I called her "Janie Osgood" because, to me, she *really* was like that character. She never left anything unturned.

Doris was really a lovely person with a great sense of humour. She loved to laugh. Once I got her laughing, she couldn't stop. I got along with Doris very well, although she could have an icy side on occasion. There were times when I would be on the receiving end of the dialogue that she sometimes threw at Rock Hudson in their movies.

One morning in December, in the early 1980s, Doris and Terry were having an argument over the phone. Doris hung up on him, and he called back. She hung up again, and he called right back. This kept repeating and went on for hours, with the house phone ringing incessantly.

It was a rainy day a few weeks before Christmas and I couldn't work outside, so I decided to put up Doris' Christmas tree in her living room. Just as I finished with the decorations, Doris came marching down the gallery from her bedroom. Just by looking at her, I knew she was still upset from her phone calls with Terry.

"What are you doing?" Doris asked me.

"It's raining and I can't do anything outdoors, so I'm putting your tree up," I replied.

"Well, I hate it!" Doris snapped. She turned and left the room to tend to her dogs.

Stunned by her unexpected reaction, I solemnly removed the decorations and lights from the tree and took it down. A few days later, Doris asked two female employees to help her put the tree back up. I was very hurt and never decorated her Christmas tree again.

I gradually learned that Doris had a knack for avoiding conflict. I believe it was something she may have learned during her early years at Warner Bros. I called it 'look and don't see'—meaning 'don't make eye contact.' If Doris was mad at you, or if you'd done something wrong and you didn't know what it was, she could come into the kitchen and wouldn't see you. You wouldn't be there. She would never acknowledge your existence.

Doris would never confront anyone with a problem. Someone else had to do that for her. Doris finally got to the point where she trusted dogs more than people.

As an actress, Doris was often times unsure of herself. She really had no idea of how good she was. She liked to tell people that she felt Alfred Hitchcock didn't direct her in *The Man Who Knew Too Much* (1956). She said to Marty, "Will you speak to him, because I know I'm doing something wrong. He probably wants Grace Kelly or Tippi Hedren more than me." When Marty spoke to him, Hitchcock replied, "No, she's doing everything perfectly. When she does something wrong, I will direct her. But she knows what she's doing."

Doris didn't like doing late night TV shows with Johnny Carson. She would always say to him beforehand, "Please don't talk about the animals." Yet nine times out of ten, he would bring up the fact that she had dogs in her home. Then, lo and behold, the next day there'd be a couple of dogs tied up to her gate, with a note around their necks which read, "Please, can you take care of them?"

In January 1989, Doris made a trip back to Beverly Hills to receive the Cecil B. DeMille Award for Lifetime Achievement at the 46th Annual Golden Globes ceremony. I accompanied her on the trip and helped her prepare for her appearance. No acceptance speech had been written for her. As the limo driver arrived, Doris turned to me and asked what she should say when she received the award.

"Talk about all your co-stars," I suggested.

"There won't be time for that. I can't talk about some and not others!" she sighed.

"Then just say you worked with the cream of the crop," I advised her. Doris liked that idea and used it during her speech.

Chapter Six

My friendship with Doris' son, Terry, was one of the highlights of my many years with her. Terry was only seven months younger than me, and he always treated me like a brother. He liked to call me 'Woody,' after Ron Wood of "The Rolling Stones." Doris sometimes called me 'Woody' also. I called Terry 'TPMD' for Terry Paul Melcher Day.

When I first moved to the U.S. from England, Terry was playing tennis every day with Desi Arnaz, Jr. I would joke with Terry—and pull him apart. He loved that and would throw it right back at me. Terry had a great laugh and chuckle. He had a wonderful sense of humour, just like his Mum.

In addition to working for Doris, I also worked for Terry when he lived on Tierra Grande Drive in Carmel. I became friends with his wife, Jacqueline. I cleaned their house and did the gardening. I was even a babysitter for their son, Ryan, when he was little. Ryan would repeatedly throw all of his toys into the swimming pool and I would have to dive in and retrieve them.

Tending to the needs of Doris, Terry and his family, and all the animals put me in a state of constant demand. Whenever Terry would phone me on my day off, I'd half-jokingly ask, "What the hell do *you* want now?" I never had much leisure time.

One day, I was cleaning the pool at Terry and Jacqueline's house when a naked man suddenly appeared. "Good morning!" he said. To my amazement, the man just jumped in and swam around. It was Mike Love of the "Beach Boys."

Terry wrote a lot of songs. He was always recording and he worked very closely with the Beach Boys. He took me up to their resort in Santa Barbara around 1984.

They had wigwams on the property, overlooking a nudist beach down below. The Beach Boys would be up there with binoculars, watching everyone.

Terry would often toss rocks up at my window in the gatehouse to wake me early in the morning. One Saturday, he hollered up, "Hey Woody! Could you come down to the recording studio this morning at 11:00? I'd like you to whistle on one of the tracks."

Although it was my day off and I was planning a trip to the beach, I went down to the sound studio in Monterey. Terry played the backing track for the song "Daydream." I was nervous as could be—shaking like a leaf. I whistled the tune on cue and Terry said, "That's perfect, Woody! You did it in one take."

My contribution to the song became part of the track that was used in Doris' *Best Friends* series on CBN in 1985-86. Later, the song was officially released in 2011 on Doris' final album, "My Heart." I didn't receive any royalties because all the proceeds went to Doris' animal foundation.

One day in early 1988, Terry arrived at Doris' home accompanied by John Phillips, formerly of "The Mamas & The Papas." John had a song running through his head and he urgently wanted to put the tune on tape, before he forgot it.

Terry asked me if I had a cassette tape recorder in my room. I said "Yes," and Terry and John headed up to my room with an acoustic guitar. They sat on my bed and worked out the song's basic structure. There were no lyrics yet, but the melody and chords were there. The song became "Kokomo," a #1 hit for the Beach Boys and a Grammy-nominated song. I saw it come to life in my bedroom.

By the time I returned for my second stint with Doris, Terry had remarried and moved to Santa Monica. But he still called his Mum every day.

Near the end of his life, Terry called me once on my day off—just to talk. I hadn't seen him for quite a while. I remember saying to him, "Your Mum's OK; she'll outlive all of us." I knew Terry had been ill, so I asked how he was doing. He said, "I'm OK." We talked for about 30 minutes and then Terry said, "Woody, I have to go. I love you." I felt Terry was saying goodbye to me, and he was. That was the last time I spoke to Terry before he died of melanoma on November 19, 2004.

Doris' home was filled with photos of Terry. They were seen all around the house and were also displayed in a glass cabinet. When Terry passed away, Doris looked at those photos a lot. Terry was all she had. They were more than mother and son. The two of them would often stroll all around Overlook, walking and talking.

While he was alive, Terry would take his Mum everywhere. If she had appointments, dinners, or social functions, he would always escort her and keep his eye on her. They were more like brother and sister.

In addition to Terry, Doris always had lots of other people to call upon, and I knew she also enjoyed her own company. She never had a problem being on her own.

Chapter Seven

One day, I was in the dog kitchen and it was time for me to take Charlie Brown, one of Doris' dogs, for a walk. Betsy, a co-worker who was nearby, thought I pulled too hard on Charlie's leash and had hurt him. But Charlie had just slipped on the wet floor and was fine. When we returned from our walk, I discovered that Betsy had told Doris about the incident. She and Doris were sitting in the dog kitchen, waiting for me. Doris glared at me and asked, "Did you hurt my dog, Syd?" I swallowed hard. Before I could answer, she said, "Yes, you did. You hurt my dog!"

I was totally crushed by the untrue accusation. Betsy was a trouble-maker who didn't like me. I never entered the dog kitchen again. From that day forward, I only worked outside and I never walked the dogs again. Sadly, it was the beginning of the end of my time with Doris.

There was always a lot of in-fighting going on among Doris' staff. The female employees were constantly accusing me of one thing or another. After the incident with Charlie Brown, Doris stopped seeing and talking to me. All of her instructions to me began coming through someone else. When I eventually saw her again, she accused me of not liking women. I told her that I got along very well with women in general, but *not* with some of the women she employed. She seemed stunned by that.

By the end of 2004, I felt it was once again time to move on. I quit my job with Doris for the second and final time. We never said good-bye to each other. I moved to Virginia, where I met my partner, Scott. Together, he and I operated a professional cleaning and gardening service. We cleaned homes, camps, and any other place that needed cleaning. Our gardening service included planting and mulching. We later moved to the little town of Surry, Maine, where we are now retired.

In 2012, I became concerned about Doris' welfare and spoke out to the media about it. She just wasn't what she used to be and she was confined to her house most of the time. I told the press:

> Doris used to have the right people taking care of her. People like me, who worked for her out of love, not for the money. But her house is full of different people now. They're with her because she's Doris Day, the star. I worry they are not looking after her well enough.
>
> A friend of mine went round for dinner recently and Doris served it on paper plates. That would have never happened in my day.
>
> I love Doris and she had such an active life. But now she has a nurse on the property and living there because she's in her nineties and her health isn't what it used to be.
>
> I know when Doris passes, I'm going to feel just like everybody else and I will miss her. I don't think there will be a funeral.

Chapter Eight

Early on the morning of May 13, 2019, I learned of Doris' passing, along with the rest of the world. My memories of her and our time together overwhelmed me like a tidal wave. A part of me died along with her that day.

Doris' death came unexpectedly, just weeks after she had celebrated her 97th birthday with her fans from the balcony of her home in Carmel. She was photographed kissing singer Michael Feinstein, who had performed at a benefit show for her animal foundation. Seeing that photo in the news reminded me of what my Mum said about Doris so long ago: "She's always kissing the men." It made me smile.

In accordance with Doris' wishes, she had no funeral, no memorial service, and no gravesite. Her friends and fans across the world mourned her passing in their own way.

In January 2020, my friend, the late Donna Winters Addison of McKinney, Texas, visited Carmel. At my request, she planted a blue hydrangea at Overlook, near the gatehouse where I once lived. Doris loved hydrangeas and she loved the way I cared for them. Donna also placed a heart-shaped, stone marker for Doris at Overlook which read "No longer by my side … but forever in my heart." Indeed, she *is* in my heart.

In addition to the many duties that I performed for Doris over the years, I had the additional pleasure of occasionally serving as her personal photographer. I am happy to share with you my album of photographs and other mementos from my days with Doris. They provide a little glimpse into what our life together was like in Beverly Hills and Carmel.

I have purposefully not shared all of my memories of Doris. Some of them are just too personal and involve too many emotions. But I can tell you without any reservation that I always adored her—and that my love for her will never end.

Thank you, Janie Osgood, for all our great times together. I miss you more than words can say! I'll see you in my dreams.

The earliest photo of me with my Mum

Me and my family (my parents, siblings, two grandmothers, and one grandfather) circa 1944

The village of Kersey, Suffolk, East Anglia, as it existed in 1932, nine years before my birth

A view of Kersey from the steps leading up to St. Mary's Church

Another bird's eye view of Kersey

My original movie poster for *On Moonlight Bay* (1951).
It's torn and tattered now, like me at age 80

My first job in a print shop in London, circa 1969

The cover of the first issue of the *Doris Day Society Journal*, March 1970

To Doris With Love, From Woody Day

The cover of the last issue of the *Doris Day Society Journal*, Winter 1977

Covers of the other 28 issues of the *Doris Day Society Journal*, 1970-77

The outside of the tri-fold "Doris Day Society" membership card

The inside of the "Doris Day Society" membership card

Preparing for a meeting of the "Doris Day Society" at the Shaftesbury Hotel in London in 1977, the year of Queen Elizabeth's Silver Jubilee, assisted by Sheila Smith and John Rainer

Me with another society member

Preparing for a meeting of the "Doris Day Society" at the Shaftesbury Hotel in London in 1977, the year of Queen Elizabeth's Silver Jubilee, assisted by Sheila Smith and John Rainer

Preparing for a meeting of the "Doris Day Society" at the Shaftesbury Hotel in London in 1977, the year of Queen Elizabeth's Silver Jubilee, assisted by Sheila Smith and John Rainer

To Doris With Love, From Woody Day

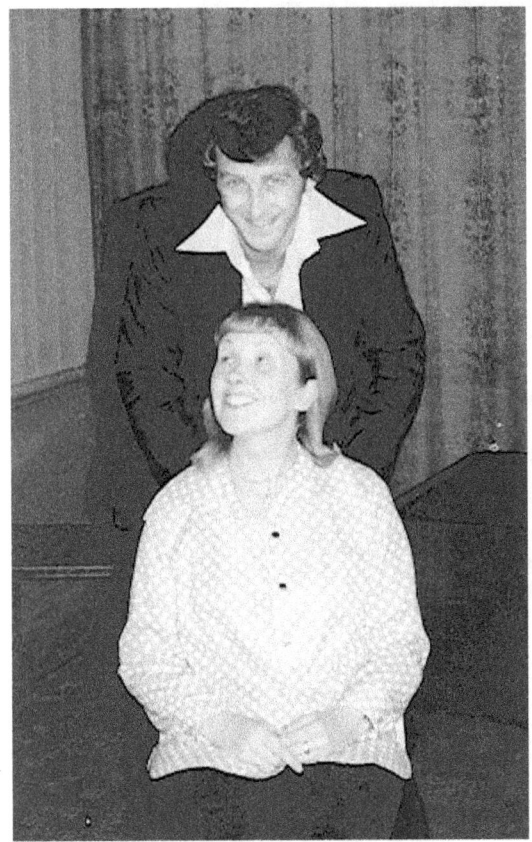

Preparing for a meeting of the "Doris Day Society" at the Shaftesbury Hotel in London in 1977, the year of Queen Elizabeth's Silver Jubilee, assisted by Sheila Smith and John Rainer

A Christmas card sent to members of the "Doris Day Society" in 1970

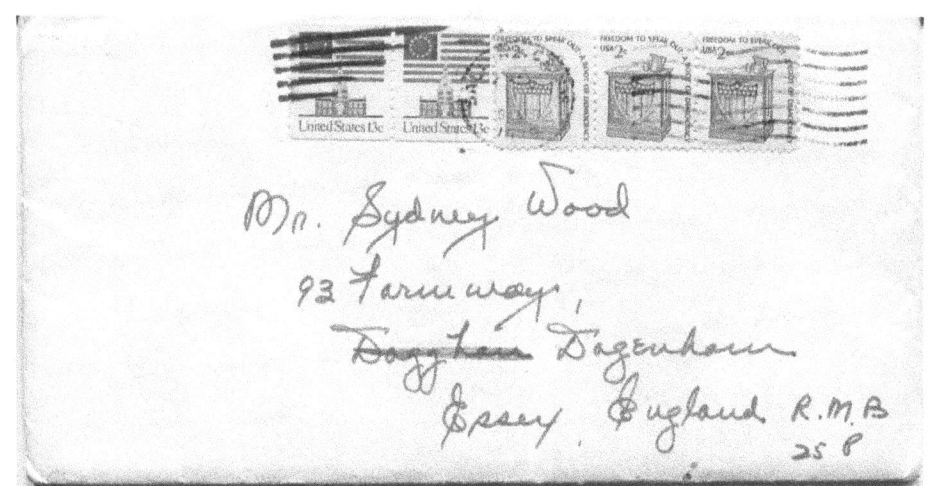

Front of envelope which contained my letter from Doris in 1979

Back of envelope from Doris, 1979

To Doris With Love, From Woody Day

Sunday 5:00 P.M.
Carmel, Cal.

Dear Sydney —

Thank you for your lovely cards and greetings!! It's always so nice to hear from our friend. We've been here just a week now and will be here one more, I guess. Things are moving along nicely and the little house is a "charmer"! By the first of June — (hopefully) things should be starting on the main house and that will really be exciting.

The weather is super — different every day which we love. It's cooler today and sunny so, perfect for us. Had a few really hot days however and I was complaining, naturally!

Page 1 of Doris' letter to me dated April 8, 1979

2/

We've been thinking about you and wondering just what to do, Sydney. It's also so difficult to put it on paper. However – we've been discussing + thinking and truthfully I feel that right now is premature for you to come over and take over the outside chores at the house. If you were to do the gardening and then suddenly had to leave for England for some reason or other – we would be in deep trouble. Gardeners are hard to come by and that place is "big" and needs attending to. Three time's weekly. So – I feel that when we move here is perhaps the time to talk about your coming over. Also the problem of where to house you there, is a sticky one and I really don't think that the three of you would

Page 2 of Doris' letter to me dated April 8, 1979

3/

be comfortable in that little apt. The little dog room would not be good either because you simply would not get any rest. Especially with your pal Rudy – snoring & honking all nite. Incidentally – he's as cute as ever but has been a little "gimpy" lately. The legs have been a little weak. However Valerie said yesterday that he seems better and that they bought him some baby socks. Can you imagine?? Would not keep them on either – and in minutes – they were off.

We are so fond of you and would feel very happy to have you with us but perhaps – the timing is not quite right at the moment. Things are so up in the air with all that's going on and it's hard to make a decision, really. Sit tight

Page 3 of Doris' letter to me dated April 8, 1979

4

think about it some more and I know that what's to be — will BE (right?) Que Sera Sera Sydney — lets see that, okay? If it's Gods will for you to be with us over here — it will happen. For now — time wise things are just too "up in the air" to make a lot of changes. I know that you can understand, so ———— keep in touch, and we will too and who knows what will be. Something may happen even before we make the big move so lets just keep it loose and see.

Will keep you posted on all thats going on here and you do the same. The time will fly by as you know. Meanwhile - all the doggies here send love along with mine and Barry's and again thank you for the cards + good wishes. Doris —
Lets hear from you soon

Page 4 of Doris' letter to me dated April 8, 1979

To Doris With Love, From Woody Day

Doris and Barry with little Lucky Day, at home on Crescent Drive in Beverly Hills, circa 1976

With Doris on Crescent Drive in 1979

With Doris on Crescent Drive in 1979

To Doris With Love, From Woody Day

With Doris on Crescent Drive in 1979

With Doris on Crescent Drive in 1980

With Doris on Crescent Drive in 1980

With Doris on Crescent Drive in 1980

With the new bird, 1980

To Doris With Love, From Woody Day

With Terry Melcher, 1980

With six of Doris' dogs in her bedroom on Crescent Drive

With six of Doris' dogs in her bedroom on Crescent Drive

With six of Doris' dogs in her bedroom on Crescent Drive

With one of Doris' dogs, a collie named Daisy June

With Sheila Smith and doggies

Pool time on Crescent Drive with Sheila Smith

Some of Doris' dogs—Barney, Noodles, Snowy, Primo, Bucky, Lovey, Schatzie and Rudi

To Doris With Love, From Woody Day

Some of Doris' dogs—Barney, Noodles, Snowy, Primo, Bucky, Lovey, Schatzie and Rudi

Some of Doris' dogs—Barney, Noodles, Snowy, Primo,
Bucky, Lovey, Schatzie and Rudi

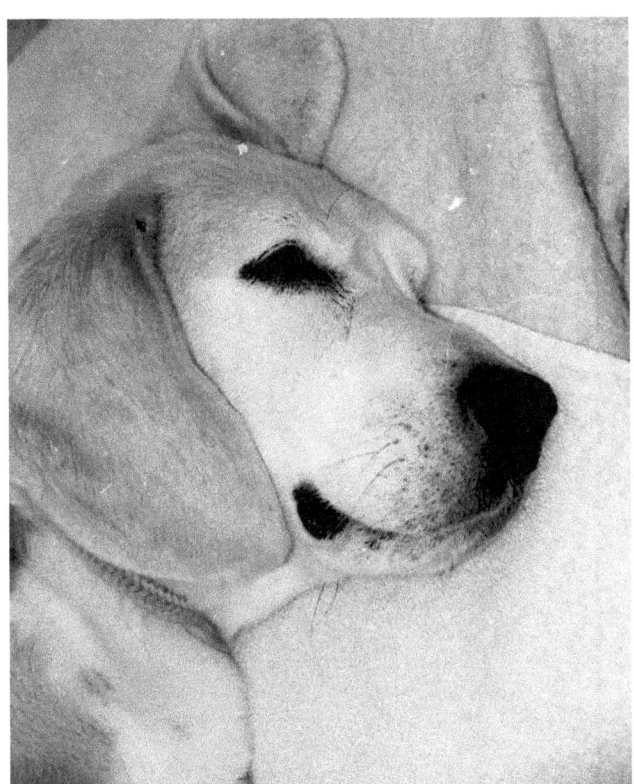

Some of Doris' dogs—Barney, Noodles, Snowy, Primo, Bucky, Lovey, Schatzie and Rudi

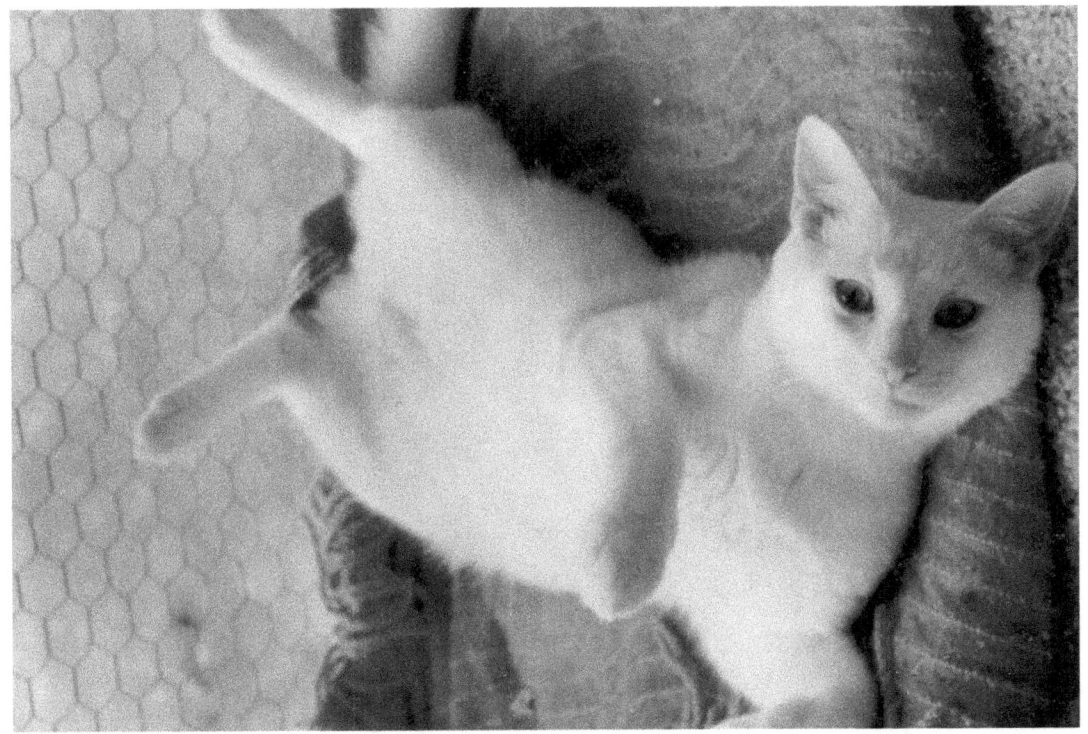

Doris with some of her cats, including Sneakers

Doris with some of her cats, including Sneakers

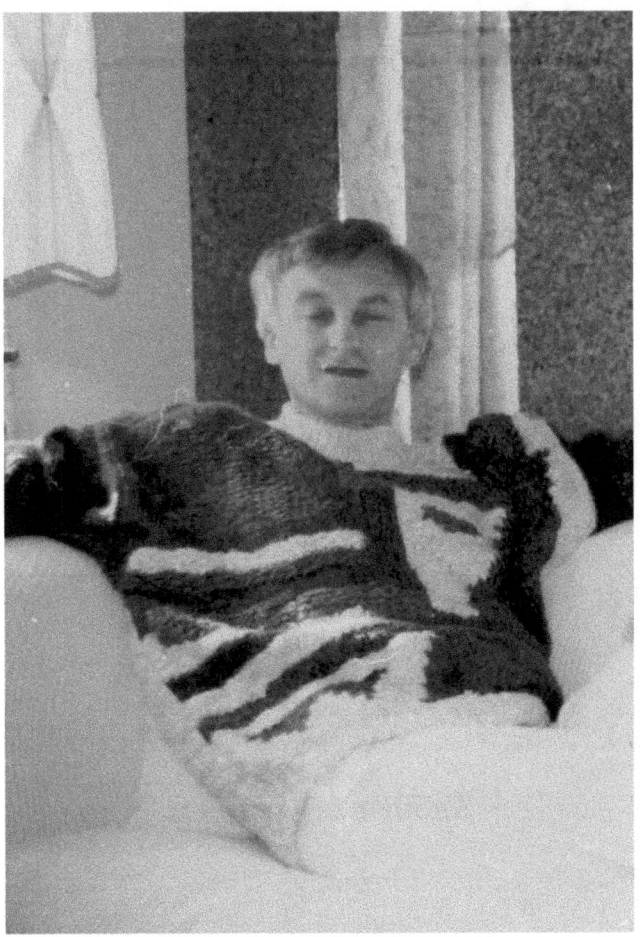

Relaxing in my gatehouse apartment with one of the cats

Relaxing in my gatehouse apartment with one of the cats

Another day, same cat

Another day, same cat

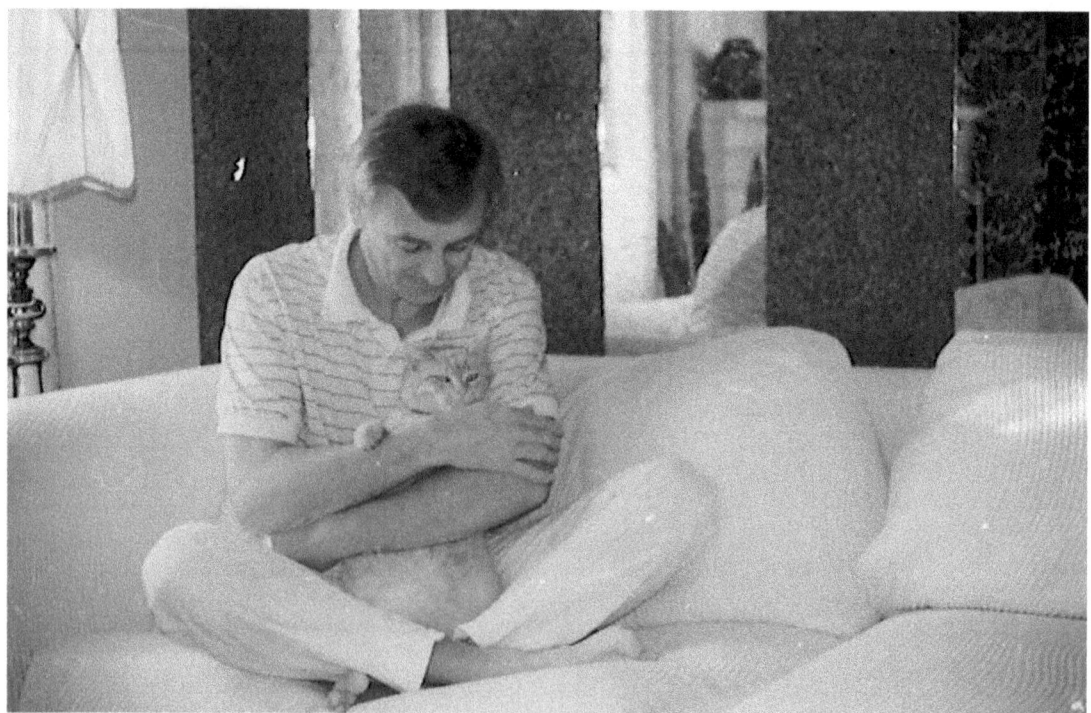

Leisure time with another feline

Leisure time with another feline

Inside Doris' Carmel property, looking toward the gatehouse

A closer view of the gatehouse where I lived

Inside the gatehouse at Overlook, before I got settled

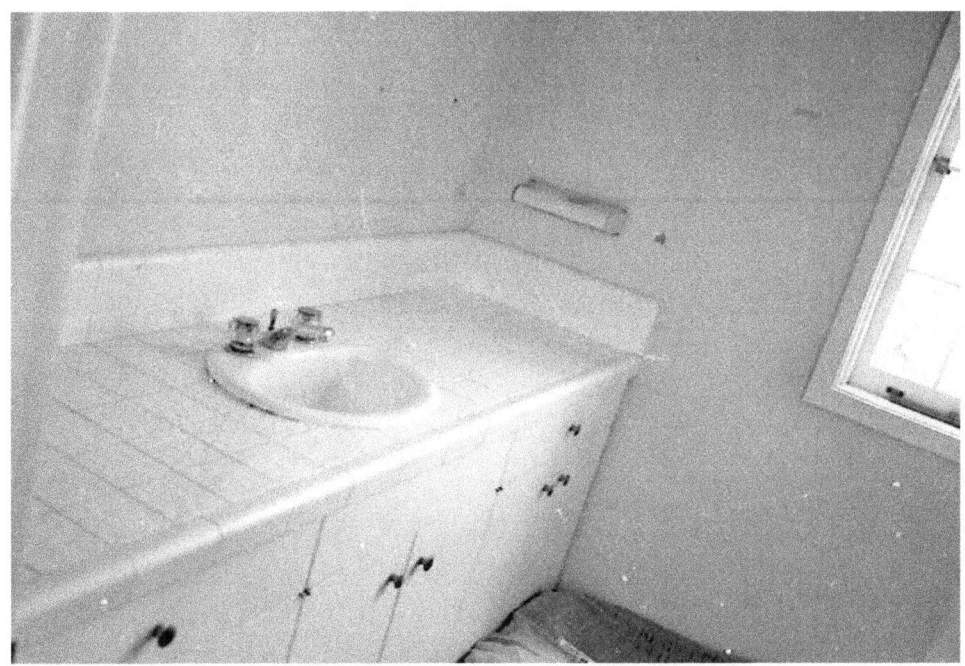

Inside the gatehouse at Overlook, before I got settled

With the brass bed headboard from Doris' bedroom

Doris searching for a stray dog

With two of Doris' dogs, getting ready to go to the vet

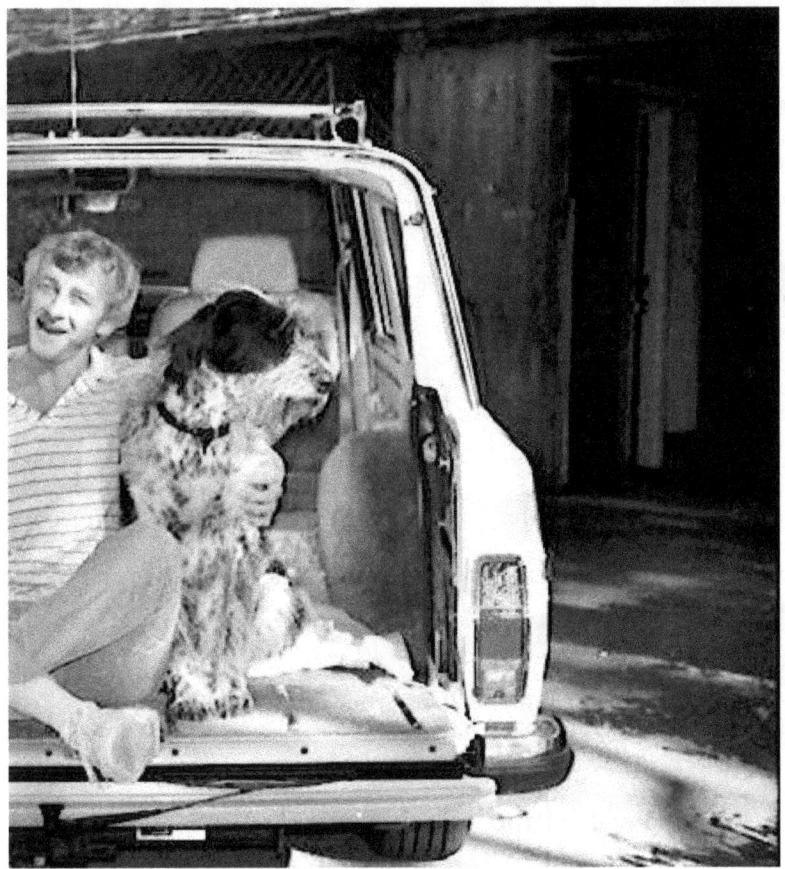

With Spotty Dog

My leisure time, which was not often enough

To Doris With Love, From Woody Day

Doris and Terry at Overlook, circa 1980s

Doris with three of her babies

Doris with three of her babies

Doris candid #1

To Doris With Love, From Woody Day

Doris candid #2

Doris candid #3

Doris candid #4, in hooded sweatshirt

Doris candid #5, one of my favorite photos of her

Doris in the meadow at Overlook with five of her babies

Doris adjusting her earpiece on the set of *Doris Day's Best Friends* (1985)

Doris in Carmel, circa 1990s

Doris with Charlie at Overlook

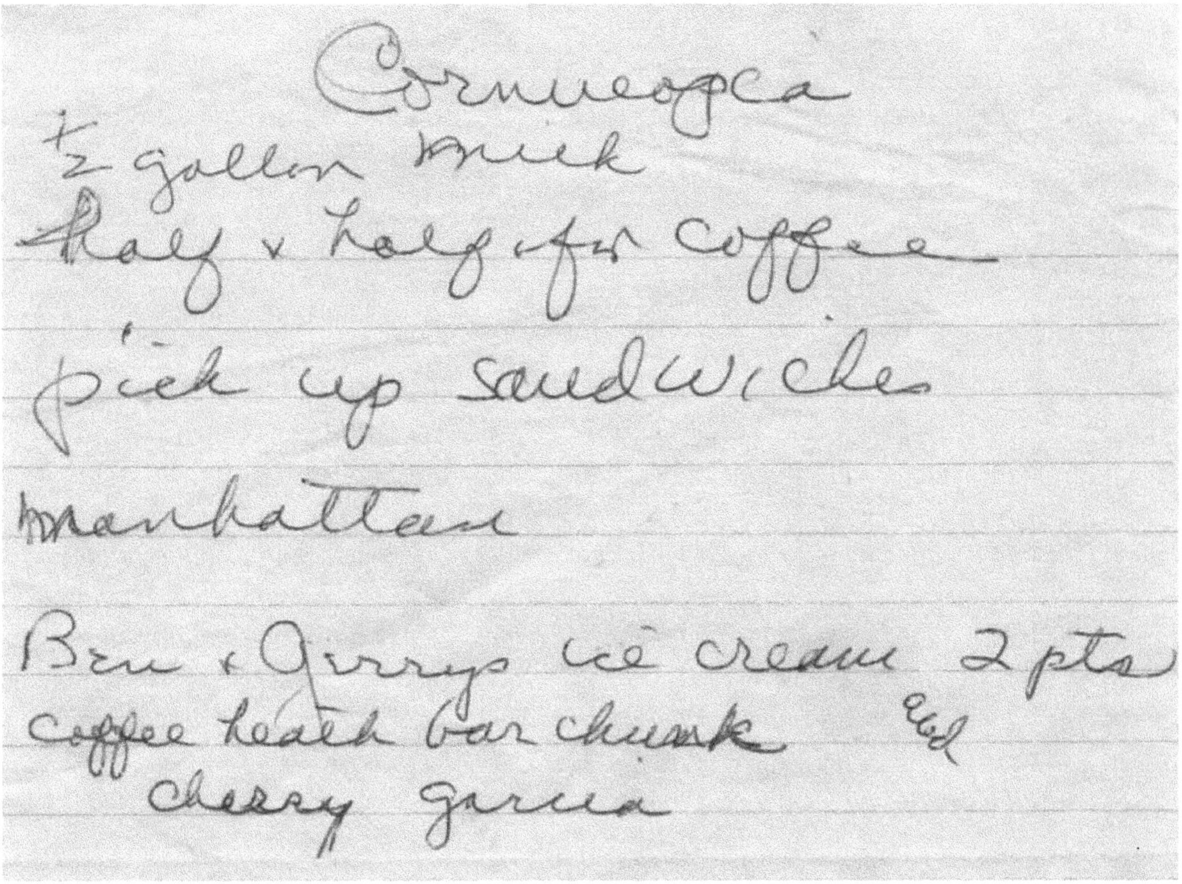

> Cornucopia
> ½ gallon milk
> half & half for coffee
> pick up sandwiches
> manhattan
> Ben & Jerrys ice cream 2 pts
>   coffee heath bar chunk
>   cherry garcia

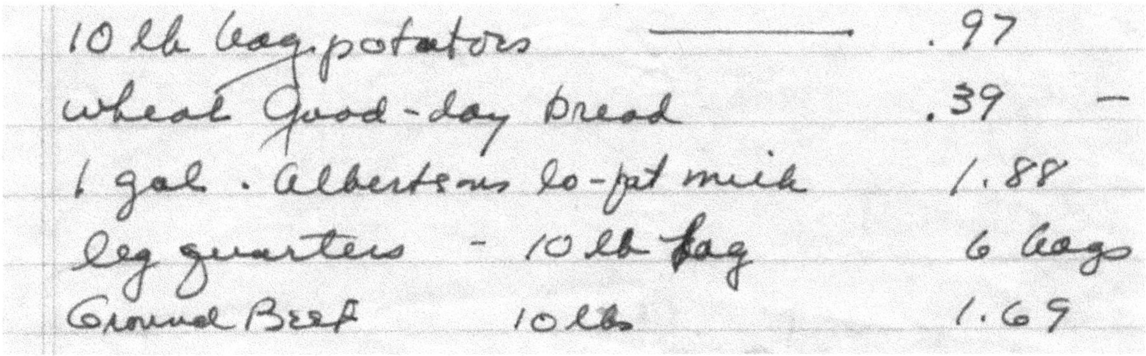

10 lb bag potatoes		.97
wheat good-day bread		.39
1 gal. Albertsons lo-ft milk		1.88
leg quarters – 10 lb bag		6 bags
Ground Beef	10 lb	1.69

Shopping lists handwritten by Doris, given to me at Overlook

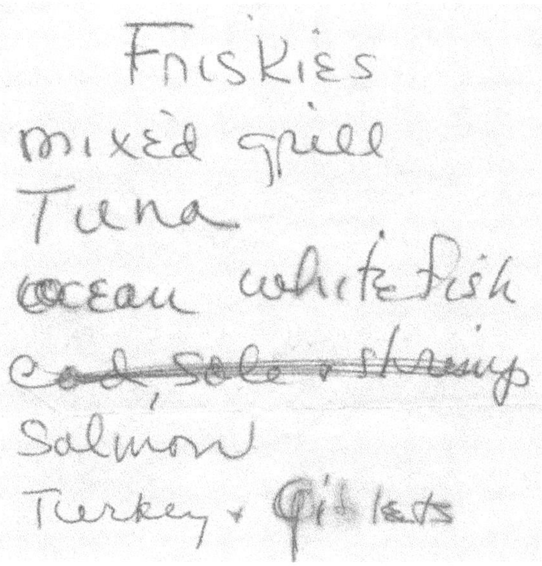

Friskies
mixed grill
Tuna
ocean white fish
cod, sole + shrimp
Salmon
Turkey + Giblets

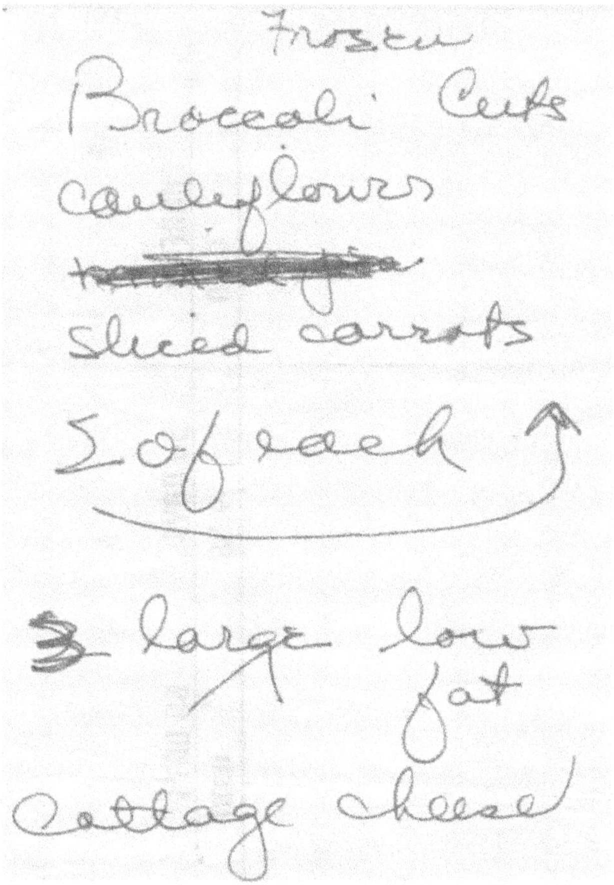

Frozen
Broccoli Cuts
cauliflower
~~turnips~~
sliced carrots

5 of each ↑

3 large low
       fat
cottage cheese

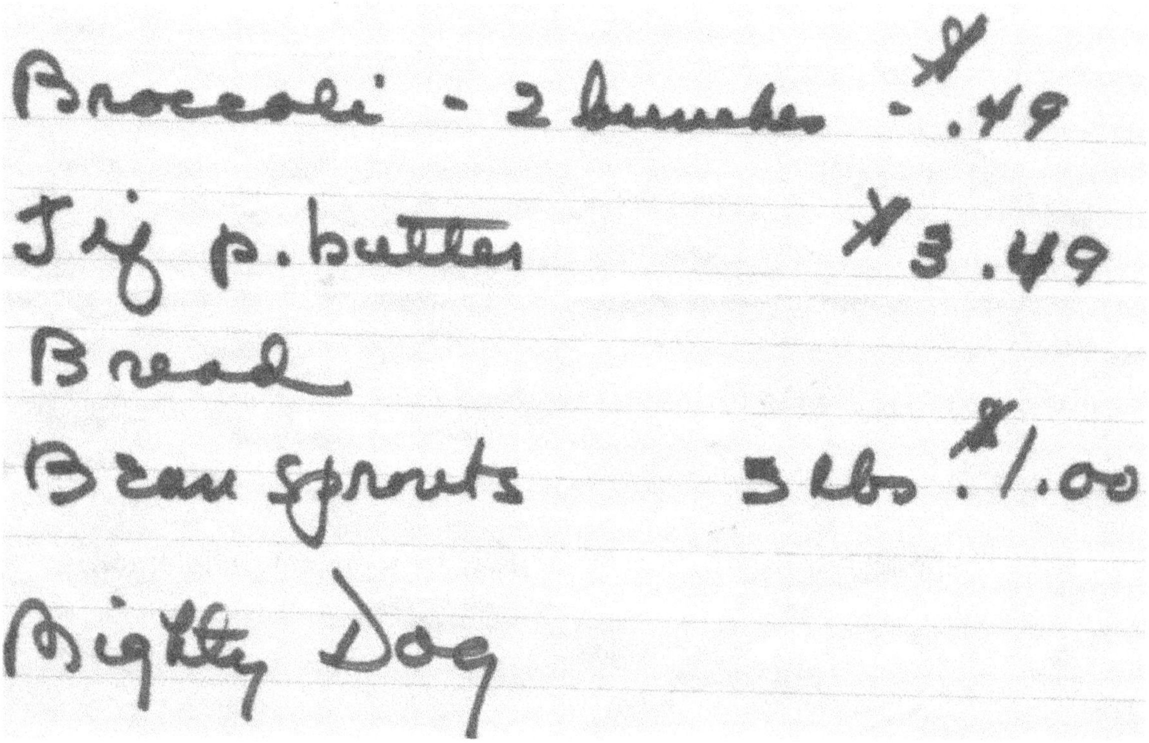

Broccoli - 2 bunches - $.49
1 jr p. butter $3.49
Bread
Bean sprouts   3 lbs $1.00
Mighty Dog

Shopping lists handwritten by Doris, given to me at Overlook

1 bunch carrots
3 bunches of scallions
1 green pepper
zucchini - a few
a few yellow squash
1 romaine lettuce (small)

1 case Natures Recipe "MAINTENANCE"

1 case " " " "Senior"

2/40 lb Bags IAMS MINI CHUNKS Kibble

Shopping lists handwritten by Doris, given to me at Overlook

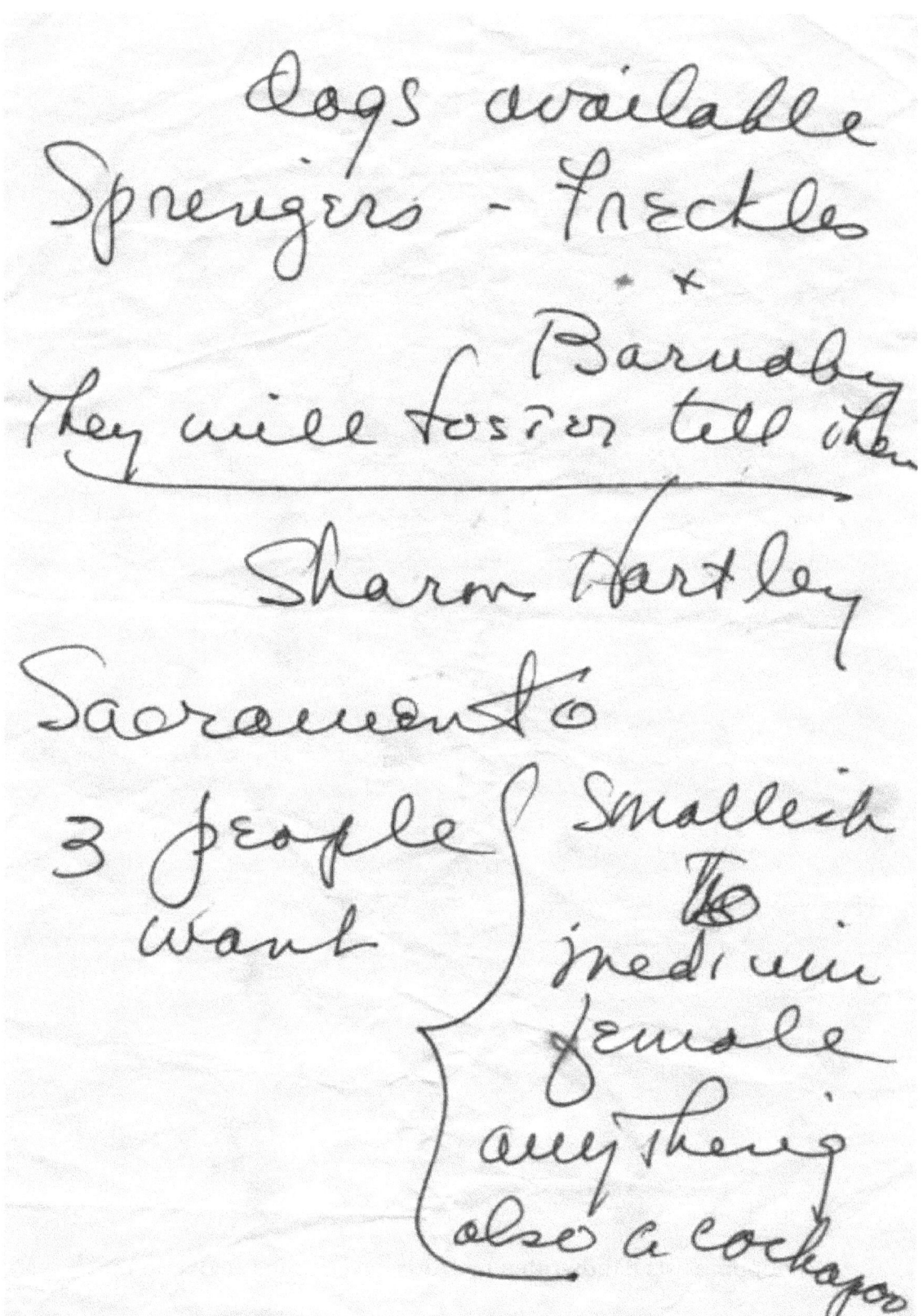

Handwritten notes by Doris regarding potential dog adoptions, a dog foster home, a pet spa, and a veterinarian appointment

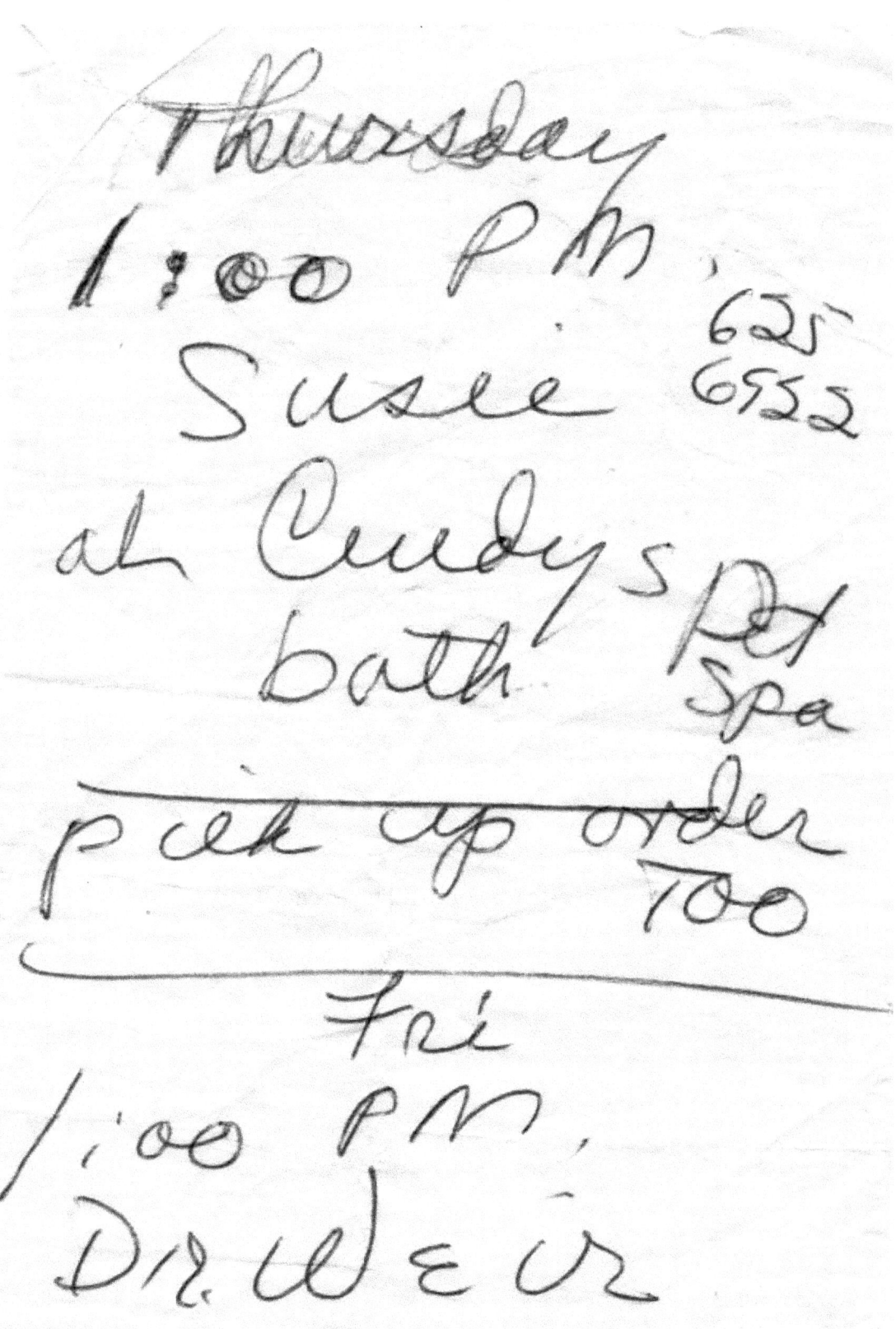

Handwritten notes by Doris regarding potential dog adoptions, a dog foster home, a pet spa, and a veterinarian appointment

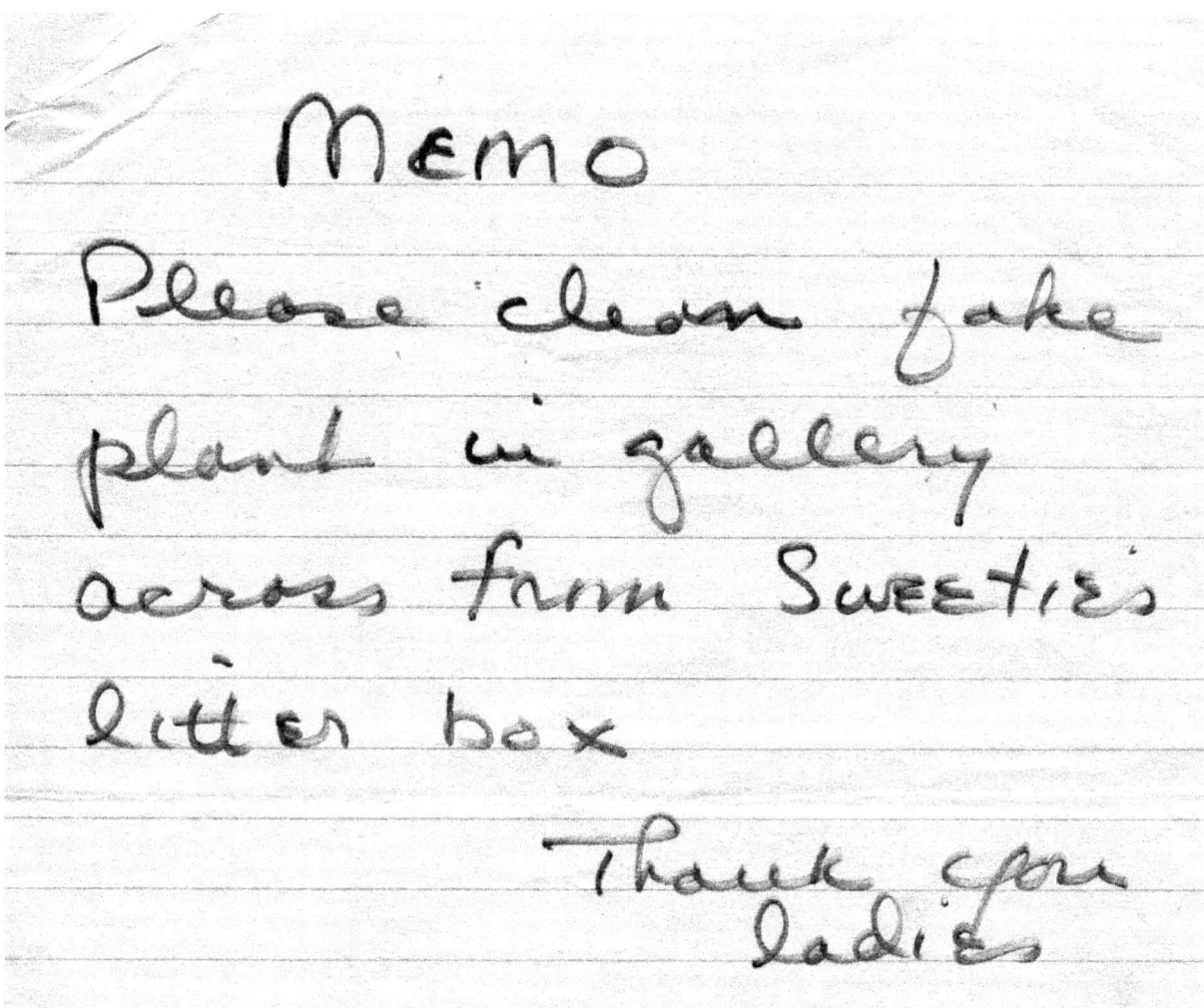

Sweetie was one of Doris' cats

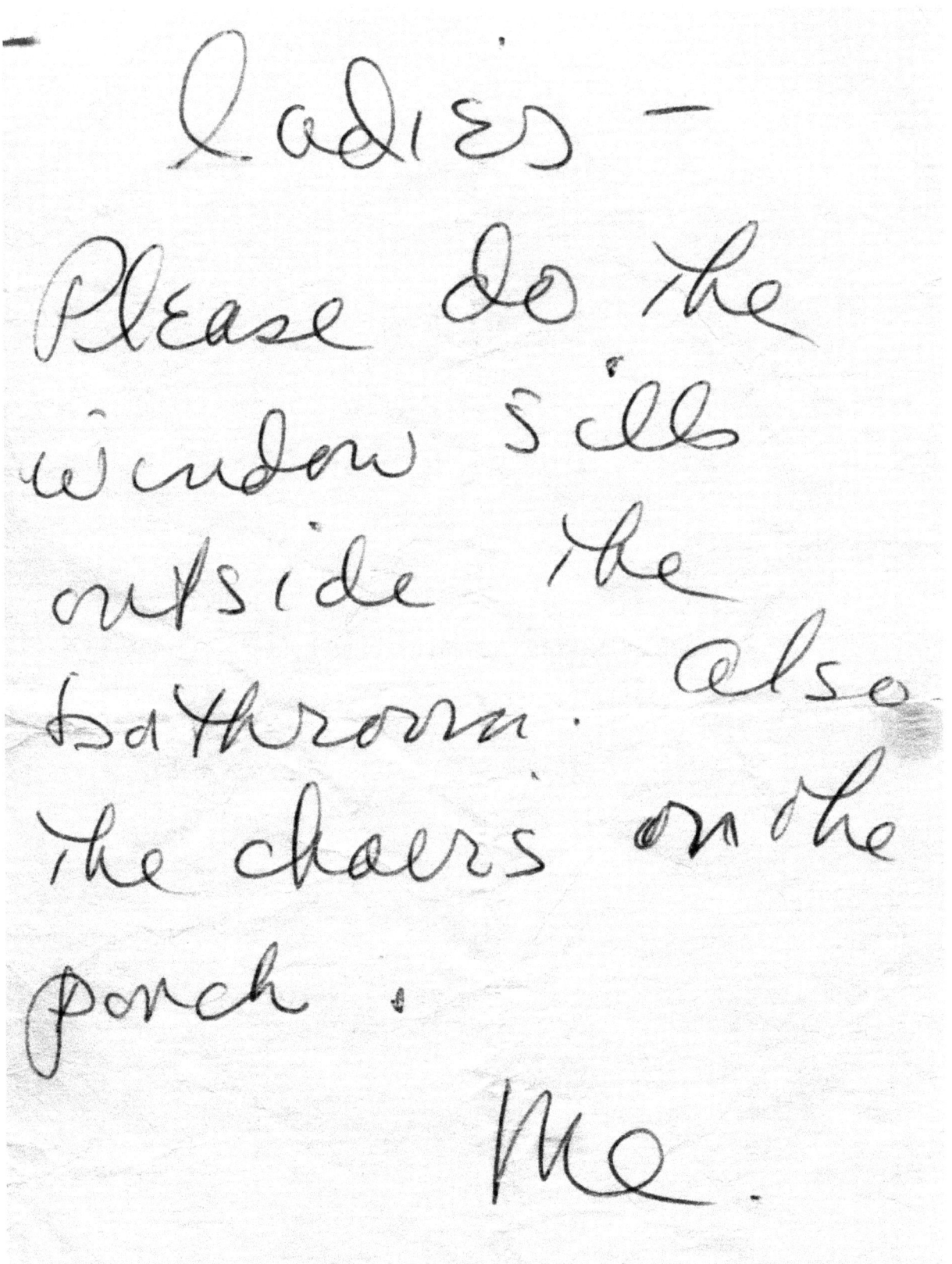

Doris liked things kept clean—she signed this note simply as 'Me'

Another note from Doris to her household staff

Doris drove her Jeep Grand Wagoneer to her 78th birthday lunch at the Quail Lodge Clubhouse on April 3, 2000, and parked by the front door

Doris drove her Jeep Grand Wagoneer to her 78th birthday lunch at the Quail Lodge Clubhouse on April 3, 2000, and parked by the front door

With Sheila Smith at The Grove/Farmer's Market on 3rd and Fairfax in Los Angeles, in the early 1990s

My Christmas gift from Doris in 2003

My friend, Donna Winters Addison, at the gatehouse at Overlook in January 2020

Doris' last address: 6730 Carmel Valley Road

Markers for Doris which my friend Donna left at Overlook in January 2020

The view from Doris' markers—you can see part of her house through the trees

The blue hydrangea which Donna planted for me near the gatehouse in January 2020. She also sprinkled hydrangea seeds, inside and outside the gate

Syd Wood

Me in 2012

END OF PHOTOS

www.ingramcontent.com/pod-product-compliance
Lightning Source LLC
Chambersburg PA
CBHW080553170426
43195CB00016B/2777